MW01621117

Ilan Stavans and Neal Sokol, Guest Curators

Essays by Ilan Stavans, Neal Sokol, and Tal Gozani

Skirball Cultural Center

Los Angeles, California

April 8 – August 1, 2010

The Eric Carle Museum of Picture Book Art

Amherst, Massachusetts

October 15, 2010 – January 23, 2011

Published by the Skirball Cultural Center and The Eric Carle Museum of Picture Book Art

ISBN: 978-1-59288-025-6 Catalog Design by Rita Marshall

Printed and bound in Italy

First Edition

MONSTERS AND MIRACLES:

A Journey through Jewish Picture Books

The Skirball Cultural Center and The Eric Carle Museum of Picture Book Art are delighted to present *Monsters and Miracles: A Journey through Jewish Picture Books*. For the Skirball, dedicated to exploring Jewish heritage and American democratic ideals, the evolution of the picture book in Jewish history and culture is a fascinating story. The Carle, devoted to the appreciation of picture-book art from America and around the world, brings unique expertise to this subject. Both museums offer special welcome and engagement to children and their families. This exhibition, focused primarily on 20th century American picture-book art is, in effect, a marriage of purpose and perspective between two cultural institutions.

Commencing with medieval illuminated Passover *Haggadot*, the exhibition highlights miraculous themes from biblical stories, imaginary monsters such as dybbuks and golems, and tales of the *shtetl*, the humble Jewish village once found in Eastern Europe. Some of the finest artists working in the 20th century are included, including Marc Chagall, El Lissitzky, Lasar Segall, Maurice Sendak, Art Spiegelman, Uri Shulevitz, Donald Sultan, and Margot Zemach.

Monsters and Miracles would not have been possible without guest curators Ilan Stavans, Lewis-Sebring Professor in Latin American and Latino Culture at Amherst College, and Neal Sokol, a research specialist and expert on Jewish culture and the Holocaust. Stavans and Sokol conceived and nurtured the exhibition, eager to convey the critical contributions that Jewish art and storytelling have made to children's literature. We are indebted to both of them for their untiring efforts to select works that create a compelling exhibition narrative. Their essays in this volume

ACKNOWLEDGMENTS

provide invaluable insights into the legacy of Jewish storytelling art.

We are also grateful to our curators Tal Gozani at the Skirball and Nick Clark at The Carle, as well as their collections teams, for organizing *Monsters and Miracles* and orchestrating the collaboration of our two institutions. Gozani has contributed the third essay to this volume, exploring the artistic side of demons, goblins, and ogres.

In addition to the artists who have made their work available, we extend our thanks to the many lenders who have entrusted their works to the exhibition: Dr. Gail Berry; Marshall Cavendish; DreamWorks Animation; Geniza Research Unit, Cambridge University Library; The de Grummond Children's Literature Collection, The University of Southern Mississippi Libraries; The Robert B. Haas Family Arts Library, Yale University; The Frances-Henry Library, Hebrew Union College, Jewish Institute of Religion; Klau Library, Hebrew Union College, Jewish Institute of Religion; The George Krevsky Gallery; Mahli Lieblich; Sasha Lurye; The Richard Michelson Galleries; The University of Minnesota, Elmer Andersen Library, The Children's Literature Research Collections; The Museum at Eldridge Street; The National Yiddish Book Center; University of Oregon Libraries Special Collections & University Archives; Golden Books/Random House, Inc.; Rita Rothfleisch; The Maurice Sendak Collection, Rosenbach Museum and Library, Philadelphia; Miranda Siegel; Allen Spiegel; The Donald Sultan Studio; Universal Partnerships & Licensing; Warner Bros. Pictures; Donna Wisniewski; and Kaethe Zemach.

Finally, we wish to thank our respective museum staffs, whose commitment and professional ideals make our work so meaningful. At the Skirball, our gratitude goes out especially to Tal Gozani, Associate Curator; Esther Yoo Swanston, Head Registrar; Catherine Aurora, Associate Registrar; Vera Westergaard, Exhibits Director; and Siena Chiang and Simonette Lowy, Skirball Museum Interns. At The Carle, a special note of thanks to Nick Clark, Chief Curator; Heidi O'Neill, Registrar; Mark Bodah, Preparator; and Kristin Angel, Registrarial and Curatorial Assistant; and, as always, our deepest gratitude goes to Eric and Barbara Carle.

We hope you enjoy this exhibition—and this catalogue —sharing the same wonder and delight that millions of children derive from picture books every day.

Robert Kirschner
Director, Skirball Museum, Skirball Cultural Center

Alexandra Kennedy
Executive Director, The Eric Carle Museum of Picture Book Art

1

THE JEWISH PICTURE BOOK: A PERSONAL APPRAISAL

ILAN STAVANS

I treasure the childhood memories of my mother telling my siblings and me her own variations of fairy tales like "Hansel and Gretel," "Little Red Riding Hood," and "Three Little Pigs." There were picture books when I was growing up in Mexico City in the sixties but I have almost no recollection of them. The only title I do remember having been exposed to before I reached the age of five was a Spanish version of *Winnie-the-Pooh*. That I can't remember these artifacts might be to some extent a result of my own faulty memory. But I also attribute it to the fact that the children's book industry in the country was incipient at the time. To this day the number of picture-book titles published annually is less than twenty. The number is minuscule when one considers that Mexico has a population of over a hundred million.

As a Jewish boy, I was acquainted with illustrated volumes that featured fables, Bible stories geared for Christian children, Christmas carols, and education texts called *huehuetlatollis* in Nahuátl. When I became an adolescent, I recall encountering in a neighbor's house a set of *Biblioteca del Niño Mexicano* (The Mexican Child's Library), a five-volume novelized history of Mexico by Heriberto Frías, a 19th-century author. In my own house I enjoyed hearing about Pooh and Christopher Robin, studying their actions attentively, following the narrative in graphic terms. But I was fully aware that these characters didn't have much to do with my immediate surroundings.

Nor, to be honest, would I have had much to relate to in the fairy tales my mother told us were it not for her ingenuity. What I most remember about the bedtime sessions was her revamping of the conventional plotlines, infusing them with a Jewish component and setting them in a landscape that included elements I could relate to. That act—and art—of reshaping the material emphasized the message she wanted to deliver. The types of trees we had in the front yard, one of which had Mexican jumping beans, showed up in a retelling she did of "Jack and the Beanstalk." I loved knowing that the same trees I climbed were part of the plot. And I enjoyed it all the more when my mother changed the title character from Jack to Shimele, the name of a friend of mine in Yiddish school. Or else, the three pigs, alone in their respective houses after having been sent out into the threatening world by their mother, were at the mercy of a threatening *goy*: the wolf. Only Mordecai, the smart pig, capable of solidly building his house with bricks, was able to look adversity in the eye.

As I look back at my mother's approach, I realize it was as much storytelling as it was *midrash*. And I'm tempted to think that at its core that is what the Jewish contribution to the tradition of the picture book is about. I'm sure parents everywhere, regardless of their heritage, do the same. But to me my mother's intrusion into the plot, her restlessness, her desire to appropriate the material is a Jewish quality. The bare bones of an old nursery tale ("Jack and the Beanstalk" and "Three Little Pigs" were first printed in the 19th century, although their roots go deeper into the past) were offered by her through the prism of a biased, targeted interpretation. My mother's parents were Yiddish-speaking immigrants from Central Europe and, thus, she grew up knowing everything about the vulnerability of being the member of a minority in a largely Catholic *mestizo* society. Storytelling was a way to insert her Jewish identity and ours into a foreign, often threatening universe.

How often did my mother repeat a particular tale? Dozens of occasions, maybe more. Yet I was enthralled every time she retold it, as if I had never heard the story before. Today I'm bemused—maybe even slightly annoyed—by the number of times my two children, Joshua and Isaiah, have seen the same movie: *The Princess Bride*, for instance. I ask them if they ever get tired of it. Their response is a smirk, as if saying: you, Dad, don't understand the pleasures of repetition. Truth is they are right: as an adult I often forget those pleasures, thinking that, as the song argues, repetition kills you.

Knowledge at an early age comes from repetition. To repeat is to allow the pupil to digest. And repetition comes in many forms. Not only did my mother repeat her stories to us at night. As she did it, she slightly modified the material, giving it a subtle yet surprising twist, one we didn't expect and, thus, felt thrilled to recognize. By doing so, she kept the plot lines fresh. She made it clear that, just as Heraclitus said that no one can enter the same river twice, you can't hear the exact same tale again: the teller has changed, and so has the listener. Needless to say, the ritual of parents and children bonding around a story is present in numerous cultures. Researchers know that storytelling at home is an essential teaching tool in the development of the child's intellectual formation. The tale is a conduit through which the child learns a moral code, a mode of behavior, and, all in all, how the world works. Personally, I trace my passion for literature to those early experiences listening to my mother.

Having grown up listening to my mother's daring retellings, I discovered books when I was six or seven. I really didn't like these portable items filled with words. I was a slow reader. Or better, I was an apathetic reader. Perhaps what I most resented was the change from my mother's melodious storytelling to an activity where my imagination was equally active but which involved more effort on my part. I remember loving a book about an abandoned automobile that a couple of kids in the British countryside decide to repair, ultimately bringing joy to their father who drives them to a picnic in it. Mexico City at the time was already an overpopulated metropolis, filled with cars. But it wasn't until I read that book—*Un Automóvil Llamado Julia* (*A Car Called Julia*)—that I paid attention to the fact that the mode of transportation I used every day could also have an emotional value. I became conscious then that children in other parts of the world lived in habitats altogether different from mine because the protagonists in that book, a brother and a sister roughly my age, lived in a town with dirt roads and lots of sheep.

It took me some years to discover the value of books. I realized I didn't need to wait for my mother to be ready at nighttime. I could do it on my own. There was a sense of privacy in the act of reading that I appreciated almost immediately. I was on my own, able to reread a page, to study a picture as long as I needed. What I missed in improvisation—my mother offering a scene I knew well from a different perspective—I gained in multiplicity: I could read not one but four, maybe even six, children's stories on my own. I could suspend the reading at any point and then pick up where I had left off. In other words, as a reader I was in control.

Again, it is unfortunate that almost none of those books addressed the Jewish elements I was surrounded with, but this is to have been expected since Mexico at the time had a population of 35 million. The number of Jews was minuscule: approximately 35,000. There was little incentive in producing locally-made books about Jewish topics. It was years later, already a grown-up (what a terrible state that sometimes is, filled with an unavoidable awareness of the blissfulness of childhood!), that I became acquainted with—and came to appreciate in full—the plentiful shelf of Jewish picture books available in English, one that grows handsomely every year. I myself had become by then an immigrant, having left Mexico City in my twenties for New York in search of a milieu where I could explore the labyrinthine paths of the Jewish self the way my mother had taught me.

Not having set out to find anything new, I encountered the Jewish picture-book tradition at a public library, from artists like Maurice Sendak and William Steig to Mark Podwal and the dynamic couple H. A. and Margret Rey. Some of their books were explicitly Jewish while others were not, and that, in my view, was enthralling: a Jewish sensibility was to be found in all of them even when their material dealt with other themes. I was equally fascinated by the efforts of established adult authors—such as Isaac Bashevis Singer—whose energy was devoted to hypnotizing retellings of old Hasidic folktales, like those recreating the mythical town Chelm that is overpopulated with dumb Jews. I remember being so enthralled by my discovery of Singer's volume of *Stories for Children*, which includes sharply-delivered pieces like "Mazel and Schlimazel," "The Fools of Chelm and the Stupid Carp," and "The Cat Who Thought She Was a Dog and the Dog Who Thought He Was a Cat," that I quickly ran to the bookstore to buy myself a copy. Since then I've bought maybe a dozen copies more because they tend to disappear from where I place them on the shelf.

Among the things Singer says in an essay that serves as epilogue to the book is that children are the best readers of literature. "No matter how young they are," he writes, "children are deeply concerned with so-called eternal questions: Who created the world? Who made the earth, the sky, people, animals? Children cannot imagine the beginning or end of time and space... [They] think about and ponder such matters as justice, the purpose of life, the why of suffering. They often find it difficult to make peace with the idea that animals are slaughtered so that man can eat them. They are bewildered and frightened by death. They cannot accept the fact that the strong should rule the weak." I find much wisdom in Singer's words. I'm convinced that writing a children's book is actually harder than writing one for adults because adults often speak in condescending ways to children, as if only adults know what the world is about. My discovery of the Jewish picture books I found in the public library showed me that there was another Talmud available, one so-called learned people seldom pay attention to, for there is astonishing wisdom in this tradition as well as astonishing simplicity.

In any case, my discovery has become a full-fledged passion. Over time, I've learned that the Jewish picture books in English I became acquainted with were but a branch—arguably the heftiest one—of the healthy tree whose roots began in the 15th century. Its manifestations are heterogeneous in terms of content and multifaceted when it comes to language. The forerunners might be the small *alef-bet* primers designed for Jewish kids to memorize the Hebrew letters in Europe before the *Haskalah*, as the Jewish Enlightenment is known, a period encompassed between the late 18th and the first half of the 19th century and mostly concentrated in the Pale of Settlement, the region in imperial Russia where Jews were allowed to settle (Fig. 2). There were also printed songs accompanied by illustrations and the *Majse Buch*, a Yiddish book of stories about legendary Jewish heroes, mostly biblical. Many of the stories in it were handed down for generations.

One must keep in mind that for millennia there was in Jewish life a prohibition against images as a strategy to fight idolatry and anthropomorphism, as mentioned in the Ten Commandments (*Exodus* 20:3-6). Truth is, there were always strategies around the prohibition. Jews living in Christian societies frequently are depicted as human silhouettes, although without faces. In the same vein, there are in existence profiles of 17th century rabbis and other community leaders. Needless to say, animals make a prominent appearance in medieval and renaissance Jewish art.

From the 10th century on, illustrated bibles and prayer books began to appear, as well as secular manuscripts with graphic components in them. Most significant is the emergence of the illustrated *Haggadah*. Some examples that have survived date back to 1526, when the famous Prague *Haggadah* incorporated woodcuts with details of the Passover ritual that included beautiful symbols as well as scenes from the journey of Moses leading the Jews out of Egypt into the desert (Fig. 3). Nowadays the modern Seder is filled with a vast array of engaging images juxtaposed with prayer, rabbinical response, as well as commentary and

2

poetic meditation. Today there are *Haggadot* for all tastes: environmentalists, civil-rights activists, feminists, vegetarians, Zionists, etc. It is easy to see the connection between them and the picture book. The roles of writer and artist are almost equal in importance. Recycling ancient material is done inventively, persuading the reader to recognize the modern overtones of the story. And the creators are aware that the material will come alive only when read aloud in a group.

Unlike the *Haggadah*, which is meant for both adult and child ("You shall tell it to your son on that day," *Exodus* 13:8), the target audience of the Jewish picture book is the child, although the adult is in charge of delivering it. The emphasis on Jewish education we are used to nowadays is a byproduct of the *Haskalah*. An interest in the scientific study of history and a desire to understand myths, symbols, and legends from ancient times pushed the intellectual elite in the Pale of Settlement to see Jewish children not

3

as passive recipients of information but as active participants in their pedagogical instruction. It nurtured an industry devoted to compiling ancient folktales from oral lore, as the Brothers Grimm and Hans Christian Andersen had done in Germany and Denmark, respectively.

Among the earliest examples of modern Jewish picture books is Lazar Markovich (*aka* Lamed, Hebrew for the letter *El*) Lissitzky's *Had Gadya*, a 1917 retelling of the retribution song in the Passover Seder that was done for a *Haggadah* but, in its conception, acquired a self-sufficient

4

shape that enabled the plot of the goat kid to be followed through text and illustrations (Fig. 4). The rise of a cheaper printing press in Czarist Russia that allowed for mixing ink color resulted in the manufacturing of an explosion of political posters, theater programs, and children's literature. Among those famous for making use of it is the father of non-representational art, Vassily Kandinsky. In Jewish circles, such artistic endeavor was equally attractive. Famous artists and set designers like Marc Chagall explored its limits in children's books with Jewish topics like *A Mayses mit a Hon. Dos Tsigele* (The Story of a Rooster. A Goat.), using a story by mysticism driven Yiddish writer Pinkhas Kahanovich, alias Der Nister, best known for his novel *The Family Mashber*.

Yiddish might well be the most important internal Jewish language ever to emerge, and as such it fostered the Jewish picture-book industry more than any other tongue. By *internal* I mean a diasporic device used by the minority in different settings (Poland, Lithuania, Hungary) to distinguish itself from the mainstream. Ladino was influential, especially in the Ottoman Empire, although, as a result of geographical vicissitudes, it never acquired the influence of *der mama loshen*. In the mid-19th century, the Yiddish press in Europe was astonishingly universal: almost every classic of world literature (from the Bible to *Don Quixote* and Spinoza's *Ethics*) was translated into it, not to mention the array of novels, essays, travelogues, theater, nonfiction, and scholarly examinations. Although children's books were also an offshoot of this literary history, they didn't develop, because most of the technological devices that expedite the process came a couple of decades later. Had the massive mobilization of *shtetl* dwellers and the Holocaust not taken place, it is possible that an exuberant editorial industry in this area would have become globally significant.

But poverty, anti-Semitism, and, ultimately, the atrocities perpetrated by Hitler and Stalin helped relocate the Jewish *zeitgeist* from the old world to the new, and the tradition of the Jewish picture book moved along with it, firmly establishing itself in English in the United States. It was after World War II that the Jewish minority became more established, keeping its own identity while having a share of the nation's mainstream culture. The tradition has flourished in English on this side of the Atlantic because of the democratic values intrinsic in our ethnicity-driven society. The formula has been especially beneficial for American Jews, who, like other ethnic groups, are welcome to be full participants in the culture without ever sacrificing their unique traits. And picture books showcase this balancing act, at once managing to stress, in artful fashion, the Americanness and Jewishness of their audience. I'm convinced that the ideals of tolerance in the United States are especially important. Tolerance was a value during my Mexican childhood. But simultaneously stressing one's Mexicanness and Jewishness wasn't something to be done in public. *Un judío*, a Jew, was a *rara avis*, a rare bird. There was no apparent benefit in combining, in collective terms, these two sides of a person's identity.

This cultural extroversion of American Jews makes it possible to create a children's art that is of the highest quality. Think of Sendak's *Where the Wild Things Are*, one of my all-time favorites: it delves into the terrain of children's deep fears in a way that is at once beautiful and unexpected. The Brothers Grimm tales palpitate in the background but there's something utterly original in the delivery of the plot line, even though the text is only ten sentences long. Sendak is an American master: his protagonist, Max, dresses up as a wolf during his adventures with the wild things. In other words, he's still himself inside while pretending to be a fearful animal on the outside, keeping his identity intact.

Needless to say, the United States, since the late-19th century, has had a love affair with the visual image in all its manifestations, and Jews have been at the forefront of this romance, from Hollywood to television, from the comic-book industry to the graphic novel, and, more recently, the rise of the Internet. Movie producers like Samuel Goldwyn and superheroes such as Superman have a distinct Jewish sensibility. The Jewish picture book in the United States makes a business of recycling ancient stories, be they biblical or belonging to other periods in history, especially the Yiddish past, like Uri Shulevitz's *The Travels of Benjamin of Tudela: Through Three Continents in the Twelfth Century* (Fig. 16), Mordicai Gerstein's *Sholom's Treasure: How Sholom Aleichem Became a Writer* (Fig. 5), and Simms Taback's retelling of a Yiddish song he heard in his childhood in *Joseph Had a Little Overcoat* (Fig. 6).

There are tales of monsters and miracles that make the reader revel in the wonders of endurance. And there are contemporary stories about escape, like the episodic *Curious George* (the Reys were Jewish refugees from Hitler's Germany who found a safe haven in Brazil before

5

If a pauper eats a chicken, one of them is sick.
Labish
Fagele
Zayn Gezundt
from Sister Tova
Joseph Kohn
Yehupitz,
Poland

Chad Gadya
One kid, one kid
Mazl-
tov

moving to the United States), or about immigration and acculturation, like Linda Heller's *The Castle on Hester Street* (pages 60-61) or Richard Michelson's *Grandpa's Gamble* (page 64) or *Too Young For Yiddish* (Fig. 11). Indeed, it's arguable that American Jews have consolidated their *weltanschauung* through Jewish picture books. There are volumes like *As Good As Anybody*, illustrated by Raul Colon, that deal with race relations (Fig. 7). Topics such as these were once anathema in Jewish circles, especially among children. Their appearance has brought along enviable openness.

I've become particularly interested in the way the Bible has been adapted for Jewish children through picture books. This attitude, needless to say, isn't particular to the English-language portion of the tradition in the United States. The first children's Bibles were in Latin during the Middle Ages. The approach, of course, was pedagogical: to nurture the next generation with religious stories from an early age. Aside from the *Majse Buch*, Jews didn't embrace it until the 19th century. Books like Moses Mordecai Büdinger's *Derekh Emunah* (The Way of Faith) and Jakob Auerbach's *Kleine Schul* (Little School) were immensely popular among children. The Bible as a source of inspiration for Jewish picture books in the United States in the second half of the 20th century is fecund, including Singer's *Why Noah Chose the Dove* (pages 68-69), Mordicai Gerstein's *The White Ram* (Fig. 8), *Jonah and the Two Great Fish* (Back cover), and *The Shadow of a Flying Bird*, and Elie Wiesel's *King Solomon and His Magic Ring* (Fig. 1).

Such has been the impetus that books and characters have jumped to other media, as is the case with endless film adaptations, TV shows, and Broadway musicals. And, obviously, numerous titles are regularly made available to audiences worldwide through translations. Given the maturity of the tradition, one might be forgiven for wondering if there was ever a time when such artifacts didn't exist. So much so that it feels as if American Jews have become the People of the Picture Book. Yet it is nearsighted to believe that only in the United States are artifacts like these, specifically commenting on Jewish motifs, available. In part as a response to translation and the impact of media, but also because globalization works in ways that foster imitations which in turn give room to original items, there are editorial industries, albeit smaller in size, in other nations.

France, for one, has a Jewish picture-book tradition defined by figures like Marc Chagall himself. In the

7

8

Spanish-speaking world, especially in Argentina, authors like Marcelo Birnmajer and Perla Suez have produced books designed for a Jewish audience. In Russia the Jewish writer and children's literature classic Samuel Marshak generates constant interest. In Brazil, Lasar Segall illustrated Yiddish books, and Moacyr Scliar is responsible for an inspired reimagining of the *alef-bet*. And in Israel, the number of picture books published on a yearly basis grows as time goes by. I own several different editions of stories by Haim Nakhman Bialik, the poet of the Hebrew renaissance, illustrated for children, as well as dozens of volumes written by contemporary authors. All this is to say that the polyglot and multicultural qualities of the tradition point to its vitality.

I started this appraisal by celebrating the importance my mother's bedtime tales had on me while suggesting that her enchanting style feels remote as time goes by. I'm not convinced oral storytelling is dead in metropolitan areas. It simply comes in different presentations, as my mother's exercises prove. Having become a Mexican-American Jew (three identities in one, shifting in kaleidoscopic fashion!), I cherish the astonishing possibilities of the tradition of the Jewish picture book available in English and in other languages. I know that tonight somewhere around the globe a Jewish parent will read a book to a child and in that magical encounter a heritage will magically pass from one generation to the next. But I know that the act of reading is unlikely to be passive.

When my children were little, before tucking them into bed, I frequently read them the Chelm tales from Singer's *Stories for Children* that I bought after discovering it in the library. My own reading wasn't passive. What I enjoyed the most was emulating my mother, deliberately changing parts of the story I came across in the book, setting portions of the plot in our home town, including people my kids and I knew well as characters. At first my children would get annoyed by the intrusion, but in the end that's what they most appreciated. I wanted the oral and the written to converge in me. For I had learned that reading picture books among Jews is an active, creative endeavor in which the reader controls the tale, becoming a full partner in its authorship.

There was once, a long time ago, a fine young prince who sometimes got very strange ideas in his head...
Father, did you know that I'm really a rooster?
A ROOSTER? HA, HA! And I'm a teapot! HA! HA!

THE STORY WITHIN THE STORY

NEAL SOKOL

Can you picture the moment a story first held your attention as a child? For many of us, books were more than mere bedside reading. We clutched them in our hands as they kept us company. Word and image co-existed in a way that both enthralled and comforted us. Each book was a new adventure. Sometimes it thrilled, charmed, or scared us, and sometimes it left us in stitches. Now, as adults, some of our favorite literary characters such as Max and the Wild Things and Curious George have migrated onto stage and screen. Rather than being confined to some cuddly phase in our lives, technology has advanced the picture book into an era where writers, illustrators, publishers, theater troupes, and movie studios are constantly finding new and inventive ways to take the familiar and freshen it.

Cartoons, comic strips, and picture books were once lumped together as "kiddie lit" or, more politely, regarded as a rite of passage, a youthful milestone, en route to adulthood, when we are supposed to shuffle off to adult pursuits and trade up for mature artistic influences. It is not as if we officially graduated from the illustrated form. The life expectancy of this storytelling format has been vastly underestimated. We now have Kafka comics for middle school kids, a picture book inspired by the writing of Paul Auster, and a posthumous illustrated poem for children by former U.S. Poet Laureate Joseph Brodsky. Who would have guessed it? Illustrated works for both youngsters and adults are acceptable nowadays, taking us in unexpected directions.

This exhibition addresses the illustrated work taken from Jewish stories that was a fixture of households and also comprised a larger part of the portable traditions that immigrants carried with them from the old country to the new. Our ancestors—perhaps even our grandparents or parents—may have traveled light, but there was baggage that could not be easily ditched. Good stories know no boundaries. They animated immigrants' discussions, their fears about being accepted or accepting, and the barriers to being understood.

For this reason, *Monsters and Miracles: A Journey through Jewish Picture Books* tells what the Caldecott winning illustrator Uri Shulevitz calls "the story within the story, the inner substance." The Jewish people excelled in illustrating scripture, in depicting the word, even before movable type. There are works that are rooted in religion but not indoctrination, in history but not piety. Inclusion of a work has less to do with genetics or affiliation (not everyone included needed to be Jewish), but the DNA of the stories themselves. And rather than treating these stories as an ethnic outgrowth, the stories themselves are to be viewed fully, each in its own right as a work of art. Implicitly, this means we have also not tamed or minimized the Jewish context of the displayed artwork. Instead, we have taken a panoramic approach to let the viewer scan and focus on whatever catches the eye.

As a result, *Monsters and Miracles* has many distinct accents, including Yiddish, Portuguese, Hebrew, French, and English, and this gathering of works makes for some surprising connections. Think of it as an unexpected family reunion, one in which distant family members each unpack their cherished mementos, illuminating how the extended family got here. To paraphrase Uri Shulevitz, we hope the exhibition will help memories come "knocking at your door."

It is astounding to think that over 100 years ago, Israel did not exist, and America was still considered to some degree an outpost of Jewish civilization, while Europe was viewed as its major hub. The Hebrew language was still in the process of being resurrected. Upon the eve of World War II, there were some 13 million Yiddish speakers. The Shoah (Holocaust) would change that forever. The Yiddish books on display here represent some of the best children's books to be produced, and these artistic creations remain a living and lasting part of our tradition. One goal of this exhibition is to take what might be foreign, or even exotic to some, and make it familiar, like those picture books of our childhood.

Take for example, "The Father of Brazilian Modernism," Lasar Segall. Segall (who in fact originally hailed from Vilna, Lithuania) is a national treasure and household name in Brazil. There are municipal streets and schools named after him, and postage stamps bear his image. In South America, Segall is renowned for his paintings, sculptures, and engravings. But it all began for him in Europe where he had forged his craft in Vilna, and later, Dresden and Berlin. As his career began to bud, Segall

10

demonstrated his skills as an illustrator of Yiddish children's literature, but his reputation on the European continent was condemned and halted for artistic and religious reasons (Fig. 10). In 1937, he was one of a handful of Jewish artists (Marc Chagall was another) targeted by the Nazis for inclusion in the infamous *Entarte Kunst* ("Degenerate Art") exhibition in Munich. The unsettling slow burn of hatred prompted him to move to Brazil by the beginning of World War II.

The journey to Brazil was far more perilous when

11

Margret and H.A. Rey, German Jews, escaped Europe's darkening landscape in 1940. When the German war machine rolled into France, spoiling their refuge, they ran for their lives to Rio de Janeiro toting with them the manuscript that would become known as *Curious George*. Once the Reys resurfaced in the United States, they began to earn accolades, even personal letters of praise, from organizations such as the Anti-Defamation League for their compassionate story lines. Of course, *Curious George* was never intended to be viewed as a Jewish creation. But one cannot forget the courage of the Reys, who along with their simian creation fled the flames that consumed Europe. Would they be surprised to know that their curious little monkey is now available in Yiddish after so many years? Is Curious George's entrée into Yiddish an affectionate novelty or an unexpected surge in a part of Jewishness previously fading from view?

Yiddish was never entirely disowned, and the Jewish artistic slump long prophesized after the war did not materialize. But it is true that Yiddish (like other Jewish dialects in the Diaspora) was beaten back. Now their artistic heirs are working to restore it. For example, Richard Michelson, author and children's book aficionado, teamed up with illustrator Neil Waldman to create *Too Young For Yiddish* (Fig. 11). Michelson explained that the rationale for his literary salute to the *mama-loshen* (mother tongue) emanated from the realization of his own children's ignorance of their Eastern European ancestors' life stories, not to mention his own lack of awareness, growing up in the fifties in Brooklyn, about his grandparents' earlier *shtetl* lives. In Michelson's poignantly crafted narrative, Zayde wants his grandson to speak only English, play baseball, and be 100% American; but luckily, before Zayde's death, the boy learns the story of his grandfather's past, which he later passes down to his own son. Michelson's book was not intended to be a primer for Yiddish survival skills, but rather a springboard to deepening our understanding of this dying language. While it is true that there is, perhaps, no hope of a full-scale literary comeback, rather than giving away one's inheritance, we pass it on as best as we can.

Who knew the Wild Things in Maurice Sendak's *Where The Wild Things Are* spoke Yiddish? These important facts and much more surface in the informative documentary *Sendak on Sendak*, produced by the Rosenbach Museum and Library in Philadelphia. Sendak explains "what they're saying are terrible things in Yiddish."

It is not that we tuned out *Yiddishkeit* or old-school Judaism, but for a time it was toned down. The Caldecott-winning artist Simms Taback's *Joseph Had A Little Overcoat* features one of the most beloved characters in the contemporary Jewish-American world (Fig. 6). The book is a gorgeous example of die-cut and collage elements with a liberal sprinkling of Yiddish sayings and old family photographs thrown in for good measure. His Joseph is based on a Yiddish folk song he learned as a child, *Hob Ich Mir a Mantl* (*I Had a Little Overcoat*). It was an interesting choice for a commercial artist. Even though Taback was very much an all-American boy (he went on to design the first McDonald's Happy Meal), he never camouflaged his roots. Yiddish was his mother tongue; he learned English later at school. His Joseph has had what you could call a double life. Taback initially created a small mass market die-cut book, *Joseph Had A Little Overcoat*, published by Random House in 1975. The book failed to catch on and was quickly remaindered. Taback did not give up on *Joseph*; he sumptuously retooled the art in 1999, preserving the spirit of the book. When this new edition of *Joseph Had A Little Overcoat* won the Caldecott Medal, Taback's almost forgotten creation was vindicated. Consequently,

12

Taback turned to the old country once again for his uproarious *Kibitzers and Fools: Tales My Zayda Told Me* (Fig. 12).

Simms Taback and Richard Michelson were not the only authors to energize Ashkenazi folklore. Art Spiegelman, a formidable writer and the visionary artist behind the Pulitzer Prize-winning graphic memoir *MAUS: A Survivor's Tale*, also glanced backwards and set his sights on the *shtetl*. His interpretation of the Hasidic parable, *Prince Rooster*, is side-splitting (Fig. 9). Spiegelman recounted the source of his inspiration: "I first thought of doing one of those "Wise Men of Chelm" stories since I liked them as a kid, but when I tried those out on my then eight or nine-year-old son, Dash, who was in the book's direct demographic, he didn't find them at all funny—just logical. So I hunted elsewhere and enjoyed finding a fairy-tale-like story with no magic except the magic of ideas. *Prince Rooster* offered two morals of wisdom without feeling at all moralistic—the notion that you've gotta posit yourself in someone else's skin if you expect to help them, as well as the idea that you can remain crazy as a bedbug as long as you keep it to yourself."

Madcap hilarity is also a hallmark of Daniel and Jill Pinkwater's work. Their spontaneity, their wildly entertaining, unpretentious, and affectionate creations have earned them the undying loyalty of children's literature fans for over 40 years. *Beautiful Yetta: The Yiddish Chicken* has an interesting pedigree (Fig. 13). Jill confessed a latent love of drawing chickens. When Daniel showed her the text of *Beautiful Yetta*, she said, "I want to draw this one!" and continued, "Ordinarily, I employ the principles of Dynamic Symmetry and Jewish Realism, with a light sprinkling of Impressionism, magic-marker style. But for Yetta, I felt a

Yetta, beautiful Yetta, will not be sold. She will not be soup.
She will not be roasted chicken on a Friday night. She is free.
She is in Brooklyn.

13

more direct and immediate approach was appropriate. First I had a look at a sketchbook belonging to my great-grandmother, Miriam, which had some lovely chicken drawings, and also recipes. Then I thumbed through my well-worn copy of works of Toulouse-Lautrec, and I was ready to embark."

For Daniel, considerations of translation, transliteration, and orthography made it essential that the story itself be quite simple, and for him, "picture books are at least as much about pictures as about being books. As she has done so many times, Jill took what was no more than a novelty, and made it into a beautiful work of art." Through Yetta's Brooklyn, the Pinkwaters have played their part in showing that a whimsical look into the vanishing world of the Yiddish speaker does not have to be formulaic.

Maurice Sendak, a Brooklyn native and first-generation American, was raised on tales from the *shtetl*. His parents immigrated from outside of Warsaw before World War I. Sendak used his family as a potent source of inspiration. In his artistic collaboration with his father, Philip, Sendak's astounding empathy and alertness to the plight of the Jewish immigrant disarm without pacifying the reader with prettiness.

Richard Michelson's book with the artist Barry Moser, *Grandpa's Gamble*, is based in part on his grandfather, a gambler, who "later found religion after he made a bet with God. (page 64)" His grandfather's parents had been murdered in Poland. But as Richard explained, "I wanted to avoid the murders and pass on some hope, though not sugar-coated." Thus, Richard has gracefully handled a potentially messy emotional subject matter.

Sendak's collaboration with playwright Tony Kushner on *Brundibar*, placed Sendak in the position of having "to confront his own story of a childhood shattered by the

AND BRUNDIBAR CRANKED HIS HURDYGURDY A MIGHTY CRANK, AND FR
LITTLE CHILDREN, HOW I HATE 'EM
HOW I WISH THE BEDBUGS ATE 'E
HOW THEIR PARENTS OVERRATE 'EM
IF THEY'RE RUDE EXTERMINATE 'EM

DEEP DOWN IN HIS BIG JIGGLY BELLY BASS NOTES BELLOWED FORTH:
NASTY LITTLE CHILD REN, QUIET!
DON'T BE LOUD DON'T EVEN TRY IT!
YOU'LL FIND OUT WHAT TROUBLES ARE!
IF YOU BOTHER BRUNDIBAR!
31
14

15

Holocaust." His aunts, uncles, and other loved ones were killed during the Shoah. Sendak's source material, *Brundibar*, was a children's opera composed by Hans Krása and Adolf Hoffmeister in 1938. The Opera was performed by a cast of children imprisoned in the Theresienstadt concentration camp, many of whom were deported to and died at Auschwitz. For his version of Brundibar the organ grinder, Sendak conceived the villain as Hitler himself, but then decided to "reinvent the character until he became a Napoleonic monstrosity." Sendak and Kushner's staging of *Brundibar* was hypnotic; its symbolism was both mesmerizing and heavy with the weight of history (Fig. 14).

It is almost understandable that some Jews who grew up in Post-War Europe feel mortified, even allergic, to war and nationalism. The illustrator Serge Bloch is known through Europe as the creator of the adorable hero Sam Sam. But his work *The Enemy* intelligently addresses war in hopes that it might perish (Fig. 15). Serge wrote, "I was born in Alsace about ten years after the end of World War II. Therefore my family comes from this unique region over which France and Germany fought throughout three wars and where one's nationality would change from one generation to the next. Hence one can find photographs of my great-grandfather wearing a French uniform dating back to 1870 and some of my grandfathers and great uncles wearing German uniforms during World War I. As for my father, one can find photographs of him wearing a uniform of the French cavalry when he was fighting in World War II. This naturally leads me to be rather cautious regarding any kind of patriotism, all the more so since my family is Jewish. Although they fought alongside the Germans during World War I, they were forced to run and hide during the Second World War, hunted down by the very same people for whom they had fought. These are the main reasons why I am particularly fond of the book *The Enemy.* I feel it has its own way of revealing how absurd these wars were, along with propaganda and the demonization of others."

World War II would not put an end to all wars, but

neither did it put an end, as some feared, to Jewishness. To the contrary, Judaism has thrived through the resilience and humor of the Jewish people. Lisa Brown and her husband Daniel Handler have known for years how to put such dreadful scenarios in their place: a pinch of levity is needed. Lisa noted that, "*The Latke Who Couldn't Stop Screaming* was born of what I like to call the 'Jew in Winter Phenomenon'—the feeling that many American Jews have, no matter how secular their upbringing and how deeply American they feel, that from Thanksgiving through December 25th, when the Christmas spirit so dominates the American market and psyche, anyone who doesn't celebrate Christmas cannot help but feel out in the cold. I was no exception, and neither was my husband Daniel Handler (aka Lemony Snicket). From this angst, a latke was born.

"The style that I chose for the book's art was inspired by a mid-century, 1950s aesthetic. I wanted it to look clean and sharp and sparse and flat (like a pancake), and I wanted it to look as much like clip art as possible. I wanted the icons of the holiday season portrayed in the book (candy cane, colored lights, a Christmas tree) to appear to be just that: icons, often cut and pasted into prefabricated situations. The same latke, the same anger, over and over and over in the face of pretty much the same frustration over thousands of years."

Of course, from Lemony Snicket and his wife, one expects, tongue in cheek, an unmatched instinct for understanding what makes unfortunate events tick. They can be counted on for taking something negative and making it seem positive and poignant. The stories surveyed here are not the last word, or even the final chapter, on Jewish picture books. There are so many stories that we can look forward to; we will never find ourselves backed into a corner, retreating into some kind of ethnic provincialism in decline. The prognosis is not grim, although it can be occasionally gothic. The stories here can be ancient, but are also accessibly alive and touching, and if anything timeless.

It is possible to drift for a while before encountering Uri Shulevitz's *The Travels of Benjamin of Tudela: Through Three Continents in the Twelfth Century*, a work for which he was awarded both a Guggenheim to write the book and the National Jewish Book Award for the finished product (Fig. 16). It is a book about the greatest Jewish traveler of the medieval ages. When Shulevitz decided to explore his childhood, he created in turn some of his strongest and most intimate work to date:

16

Dear Friends, Memories came knocking at my door a couple of years ago. My memories from my childhood. I welcomed them into my notebooks. There they sat, waiting patiently their turn...In September 1939 my world turned upside down. Fire, destruction were all around us. Buildings crumbling to dust. The blitz over Warsaw. World War II. Panic, fear, uncertainty. The Nazis marching into Warsaw. My parents and I escaping to Russia. I was four years old. We spent the war years in Central Asia, in the city of Turkestan. This saved our lives, but the price was years of hunger and misery. Now, how was I to fit this large picture into a small picture book?"

17

Astoundingly, this Caldecott-winning artist didn't have any books until he was ten years old. He hadn't even seen his first picture book until he was about twenty-seven. Before he made beautiful books, he experienced the German Blitz. He remembers the speed of destruction: his mother standing in line for bread, and then suddenly shrapnel and bodies were everywhere. Somehow his mother was spared. It was a miracle. He remembers a bomb falling into the stairwell of the very same apartment building that is the setting of his recent work, *When I Wore My Sailor Suit* (Fig. 17).

Shulevitz became famous in America for his books, but English was his sixth language. He spoke Polish, Russian,

18

Yiddish, French, and Hebrew first. Perhaps this accounts for his scintillating handling of imagery and his carefully sensitive composition of words. As an artist he has tackled epics and small wonders with equal aplomb. Shulevitz is one of the last living links to the Jewish creativity of pre-war Europe. His love of cinema and comics was nurtured in post-war Paris, where he also devoured the books of Alexandre Dumas. He drew his own comic books. And then in 1949, he moved to Israel with his family. He served in the Israeli army during the Sinai War. Through it all, wherever he traveled, he managed to study art. Then, as so many immigrants, he left for New York. When he composed his first book, *The Moon in My Room*, he explained, "the story unfolded in my head like a movie. I was the camera seeing the action conveyed by pictures." This is how Shulevitz creates his stories: he writes with pictures.

The artist Donald Sultan illustrated David Mamet's children's book, *Bar Mitzvah* (Fig. 18). His illustrations, he explained, follow "a historical line that melds time and history both politically and artistically." Sultan's final drawing for the book presents what could be taken for his "view of where we are today. It denotes a kind of ongoing struggle between past and present." Hopefully, that is where the exhibition will leave you, with a deeper understanding of where we are today, how we got here, and better for understanding the illustrated legacy left from many childhoods of reading.

In the end, as Isaac Bashevis Singer, a giant in the world of Jewish children's literature, once asked, "Are Children the Ultimate Literary Critics?" To put this to the test, I sat down with my four-year-old daughter to read Shulevitz's *When I Wore My Sailor Suit*. When we finished our adventure she asked, "Can you read that again?" When we finished it the second time, she queried, "When will he write another story?" That, my dear daughter, is a matter of time. As you grow, when you revisit this, you will discover another story—the story within the story—equally powerful and poignant—which will provide context for, and cushion the substance of, your childhood memories.

19

FRIEND OR FOE?
MONSTERS IN JEWISH PICTURE BOOKS

TAL GOZANI

Wild things, golems, goblins, devils, dybbuks, witches, ogres, and even angry latkes run amok in the picture books featured in the exhibition *Monsters and Miracles: A Journey through Jewish Picture Books*. Fantastical creatures have long captured the imagination of both children and adult readers of Jewish folklore. However, over the last half century, Jewish picture books have transformed these fearsome but often one-dimensional monsters into sophisticated icons of modern Jewish storytelling.

In traditional illustrated books, images played a decidedly subservient role to text. But in the existing form of picture books where the story is driven by the image and the text is secondary, Maurice Sendak's *Where the Wild Things Are* (1963) was revolutionary. Moreover, modern authors and illustrators have challenged readers with empathetic and nuanced (and often funny) appreciations of these fantastical beings, exposing a fertile range of childhood emotions and experiences through stories. Jewish picture books continue to depict these otherworldly creatures as (potentially) disruptive, all the while humanizing them with a broad range of human traits.

The monster with the longest Jewish pedigree is the Golem ("shapeless mass" in Hebrew). The Golem, a man-made creature given life by magical incantation, is most famously associated with the mystical Rabbi Judah Loew who, legend says, molds a Golem out of clay to save the Prague Jewish community from an angry mob (Fig. 20). The physically imposing Golem saves the community from its impending destruction by repelling the attackers, but as the Golem grows increasingly powerful and unruly, the rabbi is forced to destroy his creation to avoid an even greater calamity.

This cautionary tale of the limits of human power entered popular Jewish folklore in the 16th century. The legend of the Golem has been retold through art, literature,

film, and theater ever since. These retellings have traditionally targeted adult audiences. In recent years, however, the Golem has also emerged as a popular and versatile monster in Jewish *children's* literature. Prominent authors and illustrators, including Isaac Bashevis Singer, Elie Wiesel, Arnold Lobel, Mark Podwal, Uri Shulevitz, and David Wisniewski have re-imagined the Golem legend for a younger audience.

Wisniewski's version of *The Golem* (1996) features fiery, precisely layered cut-paper illustrations to depict the historically and emotionally intricate story of the Prague Golem. The layered illustrations not only evoke the ornamental architecture of medieval Prague but also ascribe a surprising complexity to the Golem's character. As the drama unfolds, the Golem is portrayed with sensitivity and humanity. The Golem is humanized by receiving a name, Joseph, and by his final heart-wrenching appeal to his "Father," Rabbi Loew, to spare his life: "Oh, Father! Do not do this to me! [...] Please let me live! I did all that you asked of me! Life is so ... precious ... to me!"

Wisniewski's oversized Golem is presented as a tragic figure who dutifully performs the task for which he was created but then must be destroyed lest his powers become too great. The Golem himself is neither good nor evil. The powerful forces unleashed by the Golem may temporarily serve an important purpose but, Wisniewski cautions his readers, if allowed to grow out of control, the Golem's unbridled power will end up indiscriminately destroying everything in its path. An excess of power is a dangerous thing that is unleashed at one's own peril.

Another important mystical creature of Jewish folklore is the dybbuk ("attachment" in Hebrew), a dislocated spirit of a dead person that attaches itself to the physical body of a living person. A dybbuk is said to represent a soul that has not completed its intended purpose during its lifetime and receives a second opportunity to complete its mission by possessing a new living body. The dybbuk will release the involuntary host body only once the dybbuk's tormented soul has been healed, usually by receiving help to finish the previously incomplete task.

Barbara Rogasky's *Dybbuk* (2005, illustrated by Leonard Everett Fisher; Fig. 21) recounts the famous Kabalistic story of childhood friends Sender and Nisson. The two enter a sacred pact to marry their children, but over time Sender becomes rich and forgets his sacred vow. Sender refuses to marry his daughter Leah to Nisson's poor son Konin and instead betroths Leah to a wealthy suitor.

21

Konin dies of a broken heart but vows revenge for the injustice he has suffered.

On Leah's wedding day, the jilted Konin possesses the body of his destined bride, refusing to leave even after Sender admits that he has wronged Nisson and Konin. Konin's tortured soul is repaired only by Leah's declaration of eternal love for him. In the story's bittersweet ending, Leah willingly sacrifices her physical body to reunite her

22

soul with that of her heavenly betrothed. Konin's desperate battle for justice is captured by Fisher's dark and solemn illustrations, which conjure up the depth and power of cosmic wrongs left unrepaired.

The mystical superstitions that dominated the culture and stories of the Polish *shtetl* also inspire the mythical creatures that populate the children's stories of Nobel laureate Isaac Bashevis Singer. Singer's monsters are different from the troubled creatures depicted in the golem and dybbuk legends. His menacing creatures of the night are the traditional dark forces of the underworld, which must be kept at bay by the forces of good.

The stories included in Singer's award-winning *Zlateh the Goat* (1966, illustrated by Maurice Sendak) and his dark tale *The Fearsome Inn* (1967, illustrated by Nonny Hogrogian; Fig. 22), highlight the archetypical battle for supremacy between good and evil. In "The Devil's Trick," for instance, a group of villains attempt to kidnap a young boy. And, in "Grandmother's Tale," a devil in disguise takes advantage of a family's hospitality before revealing his true identity and causing mayhem in the house (page 54).

Sendak's and Hogrogian's eerie illustrations expose shadowless, cloven-hoofed devils with horns and tails, and sinister witches on brooms with crooked noses and bony fingers who wreak havoc on Jewish villagers during Hanukkah, the Jewish Festival of Lights. These horrible creatures frighten and prey on innocent youths, attempting to lure them into the underworld. The nefarious monsters are powerful and cause great chaos but, ultimately, are stymied by the determined efforts of children able to face, and overcome, their worst fears. Good always prevails.

Eric Kimmel's *Hershel and the Hanukkah Goblins* (1989, illustrated by Trina Schart Hyman; Title page) shares Singer's fascination with the annual Hanukkah battle between the forces of light and darkness. In this story, the clever Hershel outwits a parade of increasingly powerful goblins that are holding the town's Hanukkah celebrations hostage. The evil spirits of the netherworld hate Hanukkah's bright lights but Hershel is able to trick the King of the Goblins to personally light all eight candles on the last night of the holiday, thus breaking the goblins' evil spell of darkness over the town.

Hyman's somber watercolors illustrate the dark pall cast by the hideous creatures' evil spell. The powerful goblins are contrasted with Hershel's modest physical stature. The faceless King of the Goblins, by his sheer presence, blots out the light in the dim old synagogue where a terrified Hershel prepares for the eighth night of Hanukkah. The darkness of the King's unforgiving black silhouette is pierced only by the two evil red eyes glaring at Hershel. The light returns to the illustrations only after Hershel tricks the King of the Goblins to light the menorah (ostensibly to allow Hershel to recognize the true identity of the demonic creature).

As in Singer's stories, Kimmel shows that good can triumph over evil, and light defeat dark. Hershel saves the town from the goblins by overcoming his trepidations and outwitting the powerful creatures. The goblins' physical

strength is no match for Hershel's wit. Kimmel's droll story educates children about the power of the mind, which can overcome even the most powerful spirit of the underworld.

Maurice Sendak's *Where the Wild Things Are* (1963) revolutionized the use of monsters in children's picture books by gently rendering his "wild things" as the innocent and innocuous by-products of a child's active imagination (Fig. 23). These monsters exist only in the child's imagination and thus are completely at the mercy of the child who invents them.

The imaginative plot of *Wild Things* is propelled forward by a series of evocative illustrations tersely wrapped in ten sentences. Young Max is sent to his room without dinner for misbehaving. A deep forest soon grows inside his

23

bedroom, and Max sails off in his "private boat" to the land of the wild things. There, he encounters frightful monsters with "terrible roars[,] terrible teeth[,] terrible eyes and [...] terrible claws." Undaunted, an angry Max tames these wild creatures by fearlessly staring into their yellow eyes without blinking. Max is crowned "King of all Wild Things" and revels in his fantasy of absolute freedom and power.

Max leads the wild things on a wordless, dramatically illustrated wild rumpus, which extends over several pages. Suddenly, he ends the mayhem with a gruff command: "Now Stop!" and sends the wild things off to bed without their supper. Max realizes that he is tired of being king of all the wild things and yearns to be where he is most loved—home. To the chagrin of his loyal subjects, the wild things, Max boards his personal boat, bids the monsters farewell, and, after a long journey of night and day, returns to his room, relieved to find a hot supper waiting there for him.

Sendak modeled his "wild things" on his own detested Jewish relatives from Brooklyn who, during Sendak's childhood, impressed him with their "bad teeth and hairy noses" and their monstrously voracious appetites. Sendak remembered being terrorized by such cooing comments as: "You're so cute I could eat you up!" fully believing that if his "mother did not hurry up with the cooking, they probably would [eat him up]." Inspired by these memories, Sendak has wild Max warn his exasperated mother: "I'll eat you up!" right before he is sent to his room.

Contemporary critics complained that Sendak's story and illustrations inappropriately celebrated Max's bad behavior. They were disturbed that Sendak featured a child's "dark side" in a genre previously reserved for more cheerful and innocent representations of children. Critics were also bothered by Sendak's seemingly cavalier attitude toward Max's uncontrollable rage and subsequent escape into an imaginary world populated by fantastical creatures. Many of them rejected Sendak's sanguine view of an unfettered childhood imagination (full of wild things) as a useful mechanism for coping with the inevitable frustrations of childhood.

Despite his critics, Sendak's innovative approach to children's stories emerged as a model for scores of children's picture-book authors and illustrators. In the decades following publication of Sendak's *Wild Things*, Jewish picture books have employed monsters to address an ever-expanding range of childhood emotions and experiences, often in unexpectedly sophisticated (and humorous) ways.

William Steig introduced the idea that monsters could be heroes by creating a cheerfully repulsive ogre, Shrek, in the eponymously titled 1990 story (Front cover, page 70). Representing the idea of the outsider as hero, Shrek ("fear" or "terror" in Yiddish) demonstrates that even the ugly and repulsive can fall in love and live "horribly ever after."

Shrek's physical ugliness and the "awful fumes" he exudes frighten off most living creatures and render him a social outcast. But his rude demeanor and revolting presence are matched by an equally great determination and courage to find a soul mate "even uglier than [Shrek]." Shrek always maintains his "rabid self-esteem," yodeling to himself that he was "happier than ever to be exactly what he was" after realizing that the hideously frightening creatures he sees reflected in the Hall of Mirrors are "ALL ME!"

24

Steig's vibrantly colorful and funny illustrations depict a protagonist who is lovable without being cuddly, good-natured but not friendly, ugly and yet projecting a positive self-image. Shrek makes the perfect anti-hero, socially rejected for his physical repugnance but able to experience the kind of true love and happiness that so often eludes those bound by ordinary social conventions. *Shrek!* models the importance of being comfortable in one's own skin and defies the traditional fairytale notion that love and happiness are only for the young and the beautiful (cover and page 70).

In *The Demons' Mistake: A Story from Chelm* (2000, illustrated by Mark Podwal; Fig. 24), Francine Prose similarly chooses unusual protagonists for her quasi-human tale

25

of modern dislocation and self-reinvention. Prose's story spotlights the adventures of a group of demons from the Polish town of Chelm, whose sole ambition is to cause mischief. When the demons get bored with causing mayhem in tiny Chelm, they decide to bring their destructive proclivities to New York.

Sadly for them, the constant hustle and bustle of New York interferes with the demons' ability to practice their tried and true forms of mischief. But eventually they learn to adapt their tricks to their new big city environment, discovering "how to get into people's computers and make awful things appear on the screen" and to misalign traffic lights and cause people to arrive late to work.

Podwal's playful pictures humanize the demons by depicting the world as *they* see it, as a canvas created for their mischief. Like human beings, the demons struggle to find their place in a rapidly changing world. But in the face of considerable obstacles and frustrations, the demons manage to stay true to themselves and happily discover that they remain relevant in the modern world.

Lemony Snicket's unconventional winter holiday story, *The Latke that Couldn't Stop Screaming* (2007, illustrated by Lisa Brown; Fig. 25), follows the traumatic journey of a Jewish potato pancake, who tries to make sense of his role in a season defined by Christmas. The iconic symbol of Hanukkah escapes from a frying pan and screams his way down the street, trying to figure out where he fits in. Christmas lights mockingly suggest the fried potato be served alongside a Christmas ham as "basically hash browns." A Christmas tree mistakes the latke for a holiday present. And a candy cane dismisses the latke's mouthwatering smell as spoiling its own seductive peppermint scent. Finally, the latke is delighted to be found by a family that recognizes his delicious purpose ... and eats him in the true spirit of Hanukkah!

To capture the sharp contrast between the self-assured icons of Christmas and the angst-ridden latke, Brown hand draws the imperfect latke against a flat background of computer-generated Christmas imagery. The latke is portrayed as a self-conscious outsider who must navigate his place in the world. The small latke heroically resists opportunities to become yet another Christmas tree ornament or to accept the assessment that he is nothing more than a delusional tater tot. Those caught up in the Christmas spirit continue to conceive of him exclusively in terms of the Christmas holiday, even as he desperately insists on the unique story and meaning of Hanukkah. Finally, in total exasperation, he cries out: "I'm not part of Christmas! It's a totally different thing!"

The tale of the screaming latke illustrates just how far the genre of monster stories has come. Like other contemporary monster fables, it reflects the desire of Jewish children's picture-book authors and illustrators to encourage children to stand up for themselves, even (or especially) in seemingly hopeless situations.

Traditional monsters represented dark, distant, and mystical forces of the universe that demanded respect because of the havoc they could wreak. Today's monsters need not be scary or evil; in fact, because of their human traits and frailties they are beings with whom we can identify. The re-imagined creatures of modern Jewish children's picture books serve a different pedagogical function, as role models for coping with difficult childhood emotions and experiences. By using monsters to validate such common childhood challenges as social exclusion, change, anger management, and the desire to be understood, Jewish children's picture books have transformed hair-raising monsters into comforting friends.

Maurice Sendak
Preliminary drawing of devil for
"The Grandmother's Tale"
Illustration for **Isaac Bashevis Singer**,
Zlateh the Goat and Other Stories, 1966
Graphite

Maurice Sendak
Final drawing for frontispiece
Illustration for Philip Sendak,
In Grandpa's House, 1985
Graphite

Michael Foreman
"One cold morning with snow on the ground, they were made to assemble out in the compound with their instruments and ordered to sit down and play close to the camp gates"
Illustration for Michael Morpurgo, *The Mozart Question*, 2007
Watercolor with pencil and crayon

Uri Shulevitz
"And so I spent enchanted hours far, far from our hunger and misery"
Illustration for ***How I Learned Geography***, 2008
Watercolor

Uri Shulevitz
"When war devastated the land"
Illustration for *How I Learned Geography*, 2008
Mixed media

Boris Kulikov
"Did Grandpa tell you about the horrible little room he shared"
Illustration for **Linda Heller,**
The Castle on Hester Street, 2007
Acrylic, gouache, watercolor, and ink

Fifi

Allan Drummond
"A New Home"
Illustration for Louise Borden,
The Journey That Saved Curious George: The True Wartime Escape of Margret and H.A. Rey, 2005
Ink and watercolor

Barry Moser
"Jobs were scarce and Jews were plenty"
Illustration for **Richard Michelson**, ***Grandpa's Gamble***, 1999
Watercolor

F. B. Lewis
"We're walking side by side like best friends"
Illustration for Richard Michelson,
Across the Alley, 2006
Watercolor

Mark Podwal
"Sefer"
Illustration for ***A Book of Hebrew Letters***, 1978
Ink

עִזָּה־פְּזִיזָה

זָּה כָּל הַלַּיִל רוֹבֶצֶת, | עַל כָּל עֵץ הִיא מְטַפֶּסֶת,
זָּה כָּל הַיּוֹם קוֹפֶצֶת, | כָּל עָלֶה רַךְ הִיא לוֹעֶסֶת.

הוֹ־הוֹ, קַפְּצָנִית! הוֹ־הוֹ, טַפְּסָנִית!
הָרוֹעֶה הִנֵּה זֶה בָּא,
הוּא יַצְלִיף עַל רֹאשׁ וָגַב;
גַּם נִבְחָן הַכֶּלֶב בָּא,
הוּא נוֹבֵחַ: הַב־הָב! הַב־הָב!

אַךְ עִזָּה אֵינָהּ שׁוֹמַעַת, | עַל כָּל עֵץ הִיא מְטַפֶּסֶת,
בִּזְקָנָהּ הִיא מְנַעֲנַעַת, | כָּל עָלֶה רַךְ הִיא לוֹעֶסֶת!

Ze'ev Raban
Illustration for Levin Kipnis,
Alef-Bet, 1923
Illustrated book

Eric Carle
"At last she returned with an olive leaf in her beak"
Illustration for Isaac Bashevis Singer, *Why Noah Chose The Dove*, 1974
Acrylic and tissue on board

ILLUSTRATIONS

The date of publication constitutes the date of the work. Unless otherwise noted, all books are published in the U.S.A., and all works are on paper and are lent by the artist.

All work will be exhibited at the Skirball Cultural Center (SCC) and The Eric Carle Museum of Picture Book Art (ECM), unless noted by initials in the checklist. Also noted are works to be exhibited at the National Yiddish Book Center (NYBC).

Front cover: William Steig, *Shrek!*
Back cover: Mordicai Gerstein, *Jonah and the Two Great Fish*
Page 1: Eric A. Kimmel, *Gershon's Monster: A Story for the Jewish New Year*
Illustrated by John J Muth
Page 3: Eric A. Kimmel, *Hershel and the Hanukkah Goblins*
Illustrated by Trina Schart Hyman
Page 4: Margot Zemach, *It Could Always be Worse*
Page 70: William Steig, *Shrek!*
Page 77: Louise Borden, *The Journey that Saved Curious George: The True Wartime Escape of Margret and H.A. Rey*
Illustrated by Allan Drummond
Fig. 1: Elie Wiesel, *King Solomon and His Magic Ring*
Illustrated by Mark Podwal
Fig. 2: Cairo Genizah, *Child's Alphabet Primer*
Fig. 3: Moses Loeb ben Wolf, *Seder Haggadah shel Pesah, HUC Ms. 445*
Fig. 4: El Lissitzky, *Had Gadya*
Fig. 5: Erica Silverman, *Sholom's Treasure: How Sholom Aleichem Became a Writer*
Illustrated by Mordicai Gerstein
Fig. 6: Simms Taback, *Joseph had a Little Overcoat*
Fig. 7: Richard Michelson, *As Good as Anybody*
Illustrated by Raul Colon
Fig. 8: Mordicai Gerstein, *The White Ram*
Fig. 9: Art Spiegelman, *Little Lit: Folklore and Fairy Tale Funnies*
Fig. 10: Elias Lipiner, *Oyseys dertseyln: vor un legende in der geshikhte fun Yidishn alef-beyz* (What the Letters Tell: Truth and Legend in the History of the Jewish Alphabet)
Illustrated by Lasar Segall
Fig. 11: Richard Michelson, *Too Young For Yiddish*
Illustrated by Neil Waldman
Fig. 12: Simms Taback, *Kibitzers and Fools: Tales My Zayda Told Me*
Fig. 13: Daniel Pinkwater, *Beautiful Yetta: The Yiddish Chicken*
Illustrated by Jill Pinkwater
Fig. 14: Tony Kushner, *Brundibar*
Illustrated by Maurice Sendak
Fig. 15: Davide Cali, *L'ennemi* (The Enemy)
Illustrated by Serge Bloch
Fig. 16: Uri Shulevitz, *The Travels of Benjamin of Tudela: Through Three Continents in the Twelfth Century*
Fig. 17: Uri Shulevitz *When I Wore My Sailor Suit*
Fig. 18: David Mamet, *Bar Mitzvah*
Illustrated by Donald Sultan
Fig. 19: Francine Prose, *Dybbuk: A Story Made in Heaven*
Illustrated by Mark Podwal
Fig. 20: David Wisniewski, *The Golem*
Fig. 21: Barbara Rogasky, *The Dybbuk*
Illustrated by Leonard Everett Fisher
Fig. 22: Isaac Bashevis Singer, *The Fearsome Inn*
Illustrated by Nonny Hogrogian
Fig. 23: Maurice Sendak, *Where the Wild Things Are*
Fig. 24: Francine Prose, *The Demon's Mistake: A Story From Chelm*
Illustrated by Mark Podwal
Fig. 25: Lemony Snicket, *The Latke Who Couldn't Stop Screaming*
Illustrated by Lisa Brown

CHECKLIST

An asterisk* denotes the work is illustrated in the catalog

Cairo Genizah

Child's alphabet primer [Egypt, 11th century]
*"Hebrew Alphabet," Cambridge University Library, T-S K5.13. Digital facsimile from printed book; Courtesy of Genizah Research Unit, Cambridge University Library, Cambridge, England. Reprinted with permission by Syndics of Cambridge University Library

Isaac ben Solomon Sahula, *Meshal Ha-Kadmoni*, HUC Ms. 444.1 [Venice, 1546 or 1547]
Printed book with woodcuts; Courtesy of Klau Library, Cincinnati, Hebrew Union College-Jewish Institute of Religion

Moses Loeb ben Wolf, *Seder Haggadah shel Pesah*, HUC Ms. 445 [Trebitsch, Moravia, 1716/17]
*Manuscript with illuminations; Courtesy of Klau Library, Cincinnati, Hebrew Union College-Jewish Institute of Religion

Jankew Sefer ben Rabbi Judah Loeb Shamash of Berlin, *Seder Haggadah shel Pesah*, HUC Ms. 445 [Hamburg-Altona, 1740/41]
Manuscript with illuminations; Courtesy of Klau Library, Cincinnati, Hebrew Union College-Jewish Institute of Religion

By the hand of **"Jacob" Hai ben Joseph Coniliano**, *Seder Haggadah shel Pesah be-lashon ha-kodesh*, HUC Ms. 450 [Conegliano, 1742/43]
Manuscript with illuminations; Courtesy of Klau Library, Cincinnati, Hebrew Union College-Jewish Institute of Religion

Der Nister, *A Mayses mit a Hon. Dos Tsigele.* (The Story of a Rooster. A Goat.) [Petrograd, 1917]
Illustrated by Marc Chagall
Printed book; Courtesy of Sasha Lurye

Ben Zion Raskin, *Der Milner, di Milnerin un di Milshteyner* (The Miller, his Wife, and their Millstones) [Kiev, 1919]
Illustrated by El Lissitzky
Printed book; Courtesy of Sasha Lurye

Mani Leib, *Yingl tsingl khvat* (The Adventures of Tongue Boy) [Kiev, 1919]
Illustrated by El Lissitzky
Printed book; Courtesy of Sasha Lurye

Had Gadya (The Only Kid) [Kiev, 1919]
Illustrated by El Lissitzky
*Printed book
Dust jacket; Colored lithograph; Courtesy of Sasha Lurye

Miriam Margolin, *Mayselekh far kleyninke kinderlekh* (Little Tales for Little Children) [Soviet Union, 1922]
Illustrated by Issachar Ber Ryback
Printed book; Courtesy of Sasha Lurye

Levin Kipnis, *Alef-Bet* [Berlin, 1923]
Illustrated by Ze'ev Raban
*Illustrated book; Courtesy of the Skirball Museum, Skirball Cultural Center, Gift of Peachy and Mark Levy

Otto Geismar, *Haggadah* [Berlin, 1928]
Illustrated book; Hebrew Union College-Jewish Institute of Religion, Los Angeles

David Bergelson, *Mayśeh-bikhl* [Berlin, 1928]
Illustrated by Lasar Segall
Digital facsimile from printed book

H.A. Rey, *Curious George* [Houghton Mifflin, 1941]
Final illustration for "The man with the big yellow hat put George into a little boat," Watercolor, color pencil, charcoal, pen and ink; Courtesy of de Grummond Children's Literature Collection, McCain Library and Archives, University of Southern Mississippi (SCC only)

Elias Lipiner, *Oyseys dertseyin: vor un legende in der geshikhte fun Yidishn alef-beyz (*What the Letters Tell: Truth and Legend in the History of the Jewish Alphabet*)* [Sao Paulo, Bukhhandlung Mozaik, 1941]
Illustrated by Lasar Segall
*"Children in Talmud Torah," Digital facsimile from printed book; Courtesy of The National Yiddish Book Center

Georges Duplaix, *The Merry Shipwreck* [Simon and Schuster, Inc., and Artists and Writers Guild, Inc., 1953, A Little Golden Book]

Illustrated by Tibor Gergely

Cover; Gouache; Courtesy of Golden Books / Random House, Inc. (SCC only)

Nathan Goldberg, *The New Illustrated Hebrew-English Dictionary For Young Readers* [Ktav, 1958, 1991 reprint]
Illustrated by Arnold Lobel

Digital facisimile from printed book; Courtesy of the Skirball Museum, Skirball Cultural Center

Sulamith Ish-Kishor, *A Boy of Old Prague* [Pantheon Books, 1963]
Illustrated by Ben Shahn

"Old New Synagogue, Prague," Ink and watercolor wash; Courtesy of the George Krevsky Gallery

Maurice Sendak, *Where the Wild Things Are* [Harper & Row, 1963]

*Final drawing for "And when he came to the place...," Pen and ink and watercolor; © 1963 by Maurice Sendak. All rights reserved (SCC only)

Preliminary drawing for "and an ocean tumbled by...," Graphite (ECM only)

Final drawing for "and sailed back over a year...," Pen and ink, watercolor (SCC only)

Preliminary drawing for "But the wild things cried...," Graphite (ECM only); Courtesy of the Maurice Sendak Collection, Rosenbach Museum and Library, Philadelphia

Isaac Bashevis Singer, *Zlateh the Goat and Other Stories* [Harper & Row, 1966]
Illustrated by Maurice Sendak

*Preliminary drawing for "The Devil's Trick," Graphite; © 1966 by Maurice Sendak. All rights reserved (ECM only)

Final drawing for "The Devil's Trick," Pen and ink (SCC only)

Preliminary drawing for "The Grandmother's Tale," Graphite; Courtesy of the Maurice Sendak Collection, Rosenbach Museum and Library, Philadelphia

Madeleine L'Engle, *Journey with Jonah* [Farrar, Straus and Giroux, 1967]
Illustrated by Leonard Everett Fisher

"Sailors! Take me up, and cast me forth into the sea," Scratchboard; University of Oregon Libraries Special Collections & University Archives

Isaac Bashevis Singer, *The Fearsome Inn* [Charles Scribner's Sons, 1967]
Illustrated by Nonny Hogrogian

*"'O Holy Power, what shall I do now?' cried Leibel in Terror," Watercolor; © 1967, ren. 1995 by Nonny Hogrogian

"And so they were married, according to the strictest law of the Talmud," Watercolor; Courtesy of the de Grummond Children's Literature Collection, The University of Southern Mississippi Libraries

Isaac Bashevis Singer, *The Wicked City* [Farrar, Straus and Giroux, 1972]
Illustrated by Leonard Everett Fisher

Cover, Acrylic

Isaac Bashevis Singer, *Why Noah Chose The Dove* [Farrar, Straus and Giroux, 1974]
Illustrated by Eric Carle

"When the sinned and God decided to punish them by sending the flood, all the animals gathered around Noah's ark," Acrylic and tissue on board

*"At last she returned with an olive leaf in her beak," Acrylic and tissue on board; © 1974, ren. 2002 by Eric Carle; The Collection of Eric and Barbara Carle; Courtesy of The Eric Carle Museum of Picture Book Art

Margot Zemach, *It Could Always Be Worse* [Farrar, Straus and Giroux, 1976]

*"Go home now, my poor unfortunate man, and let the animals out of your hut," Watercolor; © 1976, ren. 2004 by Margot Zemach; Courtesy of Kaethe Zemach

Isaac Bashevis Singer, *Mazel and Shlimazel; or, The Milk of A Lioness* [Farrar, Straus and Giroux, 1967; 1979 ed.]
Illustrated by **Margot Zemach**
"Tam knelt before the king and spoke," Pen, watercolor, and gouache; The University of Minnesota, Elmer Andersen Library, The Children's Literature Research Collections

Isaac Bashevis Singer, *The Power of Light: Eight Stories For Hanukkah* [Farrar, Straus and Giroux, 1980]
Illustrated by **Irene Lieblich**
"The Power of Light," Oil on canvas; Courtesy of Mahli Lieblich

Elie Wiesel, *The Golem: The Story of a Legend* [Summit Books, 1983]
Illustrated **Mark Podwal**
"The Dream of Rabbi Loew," Ink

Philip Sendak, *In Grandpa's House* [Harper & Row, 1984]
Illustrated by **Maurice Sendak**
*Final drawing for frontispiece, Graphite; © 1985 by Maurice Sendak. All rights reserved; Courtesy of the Maurice Sendak Collection, Rosenbach Museum and Library, Philadelphia

Uri Shulevitz, *Writing With Pictures* [Watson-Guptill Publications, 1985]
Cover; Mixed media

Isaac Bashevis Singer, *The Fools of Chelm and their History* [Farrar, Straus and Giroux, 1988]
Illustrated by **Uri Shulevitz**
Frontispiece; Pen and ink

Eric A. Kimmel, *Hershel and the Hanukkah Goblins* [Holiday House, 1989]
Illustrated by **Trina Schart Hyman**
*"It is I, The King of the Goblins!" Watercolor; © 1989 by Trina Schart Hyman. Reprinted with permission from the Estate of Trina Schart Hyman; Courtesy of The Richard Michelson Galleries

William Steig, *Shrek!* [Farrar, Straus and Giroux, 1990]
"One Day Shrek's parents hissed things over and decided it was about time their little darling was out in the world doing his share of damage. So they kicked him goodbye," Pen, ink, and watercolor
*"'You jabbering jackass!' Shrek screamed," Pen, ink, and watercolor; © 1990 by William Steig; The Eric Carle Museum of Picture Book Art, Gift of Jeanne Steig
*"The irascible dragon was preparing to separate Shrek from his noggin," Pen, ink, and watercolor; © 1990 by William Steig; The Eric Carle Museum of Picture Book Art; Gift of Jeanne Steig; Used by permission of Farrar, Straus and Giroux, LLC

Michelle Edwards, *Chichken Man* [Lothrop, Lee and Shepard, 1991]
"Cock-a-doodle-do," Gouache and pencil (SCC only)

Mark Podwal, *A Book of Hebrew Letters* [The Jewish Publication Society of America, 1978, 1992 Jason Aronson, Inc. ed.]
*"Sefer," Ink; © 1978, 1992 by Mark Podwal

Mordicai Gerstein, *The Shadow of a Flying Bird* [Hyperion Books for Children, 1994]
"Moses was writing the secret names of God," Oil paint on vellum; Courtesy of The Richard Michelson Galleries

Mark Podwal, *Golem: A Giant Made of Mud* [Greenwillow Books, 1995]
Preliminary sketch for "Over the next few days the golem continued to grow. It became so enormous that the rabbi could no longer control it. The golem caused ruin and destruction wherever it went," Ink and graphite

Arthur Yorinks, *The Miami Giant* [Michael di Capua Books, HarperCollins Publishers, 1995]
Illustrated by **Maurice Sendak**
Final drawing for "Joe greeted the audience with the Mishbooker Gavotte," Pen and ink, graphite, and watercolor
Preliminary drawing for "Mad Giant on the loose!" Graphite

Preliminary drawing for "Joe greeted the audience with the Mishbooker Gavotte...in Europe," Graphite

Final drawing for "Mad Giant on the loose!" Pen and ink and watercolor; Courtesy of the Maurice Sendak Collection, Rosenbach Museum and Library, Philadelphia

David Wisniewski, *The Golem* [Clarion Books, 1996]

"Please let me live!" Cut paper; © 1996 by David Wisniewski

*"This enranged the enemies of the Jews. They gathered a mob and marched to the ghetto," Cut paper; © 1996 by David Wisniewski; Courtesy of Donna Wisniewski

Francine Prose, *Dybbuk: A Story Made in Heaven* [Greenwillow Books, 1996]

Illustrated by Mark Podwal

*"Marriage Contract Torn into Pieces," Acrylic, gouache and colored pencil; © 1996 by Mark Podwal. Reprinted with permission; Courtesy of The Robert B. Haas Family Arts Library, Yale University

Michael Rosen, *The Golem of Old Prague* [Five Leaves Publications, 1997]

Illustrated by Baruch Simons

"The Golem of Old Prague," Limited edition digital print (ECM only)

Elsa Okon Rael, *When Zaydeh Danced On Eldridge Street* [Simon & Schuster Books for Young Readers, 1997]

Illustrated by Marjorie Priceman

Cover, Gouache

Francine Prose, *The Angel's Mistake: Stories of Chelm* [Greenwillow Books, 1997]

Illustrated by Mark Podwal

"Chelm on Fire," Acrylic, gouache, and colored pencil; Courtesy of Dr. Gail Berry (SCC only)

Mordicai Gerstein, *Jonah and the Two Great Fish* [Simon & Schuster Books for Young Readers, 1997]

*"'I will run away,' thought Jonah, 'to where God cannot find me,'" Pen and ink, oil paint on vellum; © 1997 by Mordicai Gerstein. Reprinted with permission; Courtesy of The Richard Michelson Galleries

Eric A. Kimmel, *When Mindy Saved Hanukkah* [Scholastic, Inc., 1998]

Illustrated by Barbara McClintock

"Taking a deep breath, Mindy slipped into the sanctuary," Pen and ink, watercolor, and gouache; Courtesy of the Museum at Eldridge Street

David Mamet, *Bar Mitzvah* [Bulfinch Press, 1998]

Illustrated by Donald Sultan

*"Synagogue Clock," Graphite, tempera, India ink, charcoal, latex, and gold leaf; © 1998 by Donald Sultan; Courtesy of the Donald Sultan Studio

Richard Michelson, *Grandpa's Gamble* [Marshall Cavendish, 1999]

Illustrated by Barry Moser

*"Jobs were scarce and Jews were plenty," Watercolor; © 1999 by Barry Moser. Reprinted with permission; Courtesy of The Richard Michelson Galleries

Elie Wiesel, *King Solomon and His Magic Ring* [Greenwillow Books, 1999]

Illustrated by Mark Podwal

*"Ashmedai King of the Demons Turning into a King Solomon Look-Alike," Acrylic, gouache, and colored pencil; © 1999 by Mark Podwal. Reprinted with permission; Courtesy of Dr. Rita Rothfleisch

Mordicai Gerstein, *Noah and the Great Flood* [Simon & Schuster Books for Young Readers, 1999]

"But Lord," said Noah, "I don't know how to build an ark. I don't know what an ark is!" Watercolor (SCC only)

"Then Noah, with his wife and sons, began to build the ark," Oil paint on vellum; Courtesy of The Richard Michelson Galleries

Simms Taback, *Joseph had a Little Overcoat* [Viking, 1999]
*"Joseph had a little handkerchief," Pen, colored pencil, watercolor, gouache, collage, and pastel; © 1999 by Simms Taback. Used by permission of Viking Children's Books, A Division of Penguin Young Readers Group, A Member of Penguin Group (USA) Inc. All rights reserved

Art Spiegelman, *Little Lit: Folklore and Fairy Tale Funnies* [A Raw Junior Book with Joanna Cotler Books, an imprint of HarperCollins Publishers, 2000]
*"Prince Rooster," Ink and watercolor; © 2000 by Art Spiegelman

Eric A. Kimmel, *Gershon's Monster: A Story for the Jewish New Year* [Scholastic, 2000]
Illustrated by Jon J Muth
*"And once a year, on Rosh Hashanah, he stuffed them into a sack and dragged them down to the sea," Watercolor; © 2000 by John J Muth. Scholastic Inc. / Scholastic Press; Used by permission; Courtesy of Allen Spiegel

Francine Prose, *The Demon's Mistake: A Story From Chelm* [Greenwillow Books, 2000]
Illustrated by Mark Podwal
*"Demons in the town of Chelm go to party," Acrylic, gouache and colored pencil; © 2000 by Mark Podwal; Reprinted with permission

Fran Manushkin, *Daughters of Fire: Heroines of the Bible* [Silver Whistle, 2001]
Illustrated by Uri Shulevitz
"Eve," Mixed media

Richard Michelson, *Too Young For Yiddish* [Talewinds, A Charlesbridge Imprint, 2002]
Illustrated by Neil Waldman
*"And he gave Aaron a big hartzig hug," Watercolor and pen; © 2002 by Neil Waldman

"In my village," Watercolor; Courtesy of The Richard Michelson Galleries

Tony Kushner, *Brundibar* [Michael di Capua Books, Hyperion Books for Children, 2003]
Illustrated by Maurice Sendak
*Preliminary drawing for "And Brundibar cranked his hurdy gurdy," Graphite and light crayon; © 2003 by Maurice Sendak. All rights reserved
Preliminary drawing for "Everyone Was There, Buying Buying Busy Buying," Graphite
Final drawing for "Everyone Was There, Buying Buying Busy Buying," Pen and ink and watercolor
Final drawing for "Suddenly a sparrow fluttered flappity-flap!" Pencil, crayon, pen and ink, watercolor
Preliminary drawing for "We won't mind skipping school. We Are 300 Kids Come to Help You," Graphite
Preliminary drawing for "Brundibar runs chased by cat dog sparrow," Graphite (SCC only)
Final drawing for "Brundibar runs chased by cat dog sparrow," Pencil; crayon, pen and ink, and watercolor (ECM only)
Preliminary drawing for "They believe they've won the fight, they believe I'm gone — not quite!" Graphite (ECM only)
Working notes for "They believe they've won the fight, they believe I'm gone — not quite!" Color photocopy with marker (ECM only)
Final drawing for "They believe they've won the fight, they believe I'm gone — not quite!" Graphite, colored pencil, and watercolor (SCC only); Courtesy of the Maurice Sendak Collection, Rosenbach Museum and Library, Philadelphia

Ephraim Sidon, *The Bible in Rhymes/Genesis*, [Tel Aviv, Am Oved, 2003]
Illustrated by David Polonsky
"The Story of Joseph," Digital print (SCC, NYBC)

Erica Silverman, *Sholom's Treasure: How Sholom Aleichem Became a Writer* [Farrar, Straus and Giroux, 2004]
Illustrated by Mordicai Gerstein
*"One night, Father came in. He picked up Sholom's dictionary

and started to read," Oil on vellum; © 2004 by Mordicai Gerstein. Used by permission of Farrar, Straus and Giroux, LLC; Courtesy of The Richard Michelson Galleries

Louise Borden, *The Journey That Saved Curious George: The True Wartime Escape of Margret and H. A. Rey* [Houghton Mifflin Company, 2005]
Illustrated by Allan Drummond

"The train station in Orléans was bedlam! There were a few hand-lettered signs for missing children, tacked up on the walls by frantic parents," Giclée print

"The largest motorized evacuation in history," Giclée print

*"Weary Refugees," Giclée print; © 2005 by Allan Drummond. Used by permission of Houghton Mifflin Harcourt Publishing Company (SCC only)

*"A New Home," Giclée print; © 2005 by Allan Drummond. Used by permission of Houghton Mifflin Harcourt Publishing Company

Ilan Stavans, *Miriam and the Sandia Seed* [*Spider*; May, 2005, Vol. 12 Issue 5, pp. 25-31]
Illustrated by Hector Viveros Lee
"As she planted the seed," Watercolor

Howard Schwartz, *Before You Were Born* [Roaring Brook Press, 2005]
Illustrated by Kristina Swarner
"But the moment you were born," Linoleum printing, watercolor, and colored pencil

Barbara Rogasky, *The Dybbuk* [Holiday House, 2005]
Illustrated by Leonard Everett Fisher
*"So what is a dybbuk, you may well ask? It is the soul of one who has died," Acrylic; © 2005 by Leonard Everett Fisher. Reprinted with permission

Simms Taback, *Kibitzers and Fools: Tales My Zayda Told Me* [Viking, 2005]
*"One day, while praying in shul (synagogue), Chaim Meltzer complained to God," Pen, colored pencil, watercolor, gouache, and collage; © 2005 by Simms Taback. Used by permission of Viking Children's Books, A Division of Penguin Young Readers Group, A Member of Penguin Group (USA) Inc. All rights reserved.
"As soon as he corrected the sign," Pen, colored pencil, watercolor, gouache, and collage
"You are leaving Chelm," Pen, colored pencil, watercolor, gouache, and collage

Uri Shulevitz, *The Travels of Benjamin of Tudela: Through Three Continents in the Twelfth Century* [Farrar, Straus and Giroux, 2005]
*Cover; Mixed media; © 2005 by Uri Shulevitz. Used by permission of Farrar, Straus and Giroux, LLC
"The year 1173," Mixed media
"The Long Journey Home," Mixed media

Ephraim Sidon, *The Bible in Rhymes/Joshua-Judges*, [Tel Aviv, Am Oved, 2005]
Illustrated by David Polonsky
"Samson and the Lion," Digital print (SCC only)

Richard Michelson, *Across the Alley* [G. P. Putnam's Sons, 2006]
Illustrated by E.B. Lewis
*"We're walking side by side like best friends," Watercolor; © 2006 by E.B. Lewis. Used by permission of G.P. Putnam's Sons, A Division of Penguin Young Readers Group, A Member of Penguin Group (USA) Inc., 345 Hudson Street, New York, NY 10014; All rights reserved; Courtesy of The Richard Michelson Galleries

Mordicai Gerstein, *The White Ram* [Holiday House, 2006]
"And from the ram's ashes," Pen and ink, oil paint, and colored pencil; Private Collection
*"Adam and Eve, the first man and woman, disobeyed God and had to leave Eden," Pen and ink, oil paint, and colored pencil; © 2006 by Mordicai Gerstein. Reprinted with permission of The Richard Michelson Galleries

Steve Sheinkin, *The Adventures of Rabbi Harvey: A Graphic Novel of Jewish Wisdom and Wit in the Wild West* [Jewish Lights Publishing, 2006]
"There's a new rabbi in town," Black and white drawing on paper (SCC and NYBC)

Linda Heller, *The Castle on Hester Street* [Simon & Schuster Books for Young Readers, 2007]
Illustrated by Boris Kulikov
"President Theodore Roosevelt rode his horse through a blizzard of ticker tape to greet me," Acrylic, gouache, watercolor, and ink
"The boat docked first at Ellis Island. We sat for hours and waited to be inspected," Acrylic, gouache, watercolor, and ink
*"Did Grandpa tell you about the horrible little room he shared," Acrylic, gouache, watercolor, and ink; © 2007 by Boris Kulikov. Reprinted with permission from Simon & Schuster Children's Publishing; Private Collection

Susan Goldman Rubin, *Haym Salomon: American Patriot* [Abrams Books for Young Readers, 2007]
Illustrated by David Slonim
"Arrested!" Oil on linen (SCC only)

Lemony Snicket, *The Latke Who Couldn't Stop Screaming* [McSweeney's Books, 2007]
Illustrated by Lisa Brown

*"The latke was suffering so much that it leapt out of the hot pan and out the window," Digital print; © 2007 by Lisa Brown

"It begins in a tiny village," Digital print (SCC and NYBC)

"It was the only place not decorated with flashing colored lights at this time of year," Digital print (SCC and NYBC)

"The thing that was being born was a latke," Digital print (SCC and NYBC)

"AAAHHHHHHHH!!!" Digital print (SCC and NYBC)

Michael Morpurgo, *The Mozart Question* [Candlewick Press, 2007]
Illustrated by Michael Foreman

*"One cold morning with snow on the ground, they were made to assemble out in the compound with their instruments and ordered to sit down and play close to the camp gates," Watercolor with pencil and crayon; Text © 2006 by Michael Morpurgo; Illustrations © 2007 by Michael Foreman. Reproduced by permission of the publisher, Candlewick Press, Inc., on behalf of Walker Books, London

Jason Lutes, *Houdini The Handcuff King* [Hyperion, 2007]
Illustrated by Nick Bertozzi

"Charles River Jump," Pen and ink on bristol paper (SCC and NYBC)

Moacyr Scliar, *ABC do mundo judaico* [Edicoes SM, 2007]
Illustrated by Renato Alarcão

"Zohar," Acrylic (SCC only)

Davide Cali, *L'ennemi* (The Enemy) [Ed. Sarbacane, 2007]
Illustrated by Serge Bloch

*Cover; Digital print; © 2007 by Serge Bloch (SCC only)

Karen Winnick, *Lucy's Cave: A Story of Vicksburg, 1863* [Boyds Mills Press, 2008]

"Vicksburg Cave," Oil on canvas (SCC only)

Richard Michelson, *As Good as Anybody* [Borzoi by Alfred A. Knopf, 2008]
Illustrated by Raul Colon

*"Abraham found candies hidden between the pages of Torah," Colored pencil and watercolor; © 2008 by Raul Colon; Courtesy of The Richard Michelson Galleries

Cover, Colored pencil; Courtesy of The Richard Michelson Galleries

Uri Shulevitz, *How I Learned Geography* [Farrar, Straus and Giroux, 2008]

*"When war devastated the land," Mixed media; © 2008 by Uri Shulevitz. Used by permission of Farrar, Straus and Giroux, LLC.

*"And so I spent enchanted hours far, far from our hunger and misery," Watercolor; © 2008 by Uri Shulevitz. Used by permission of Farrar, Straus and Giroux, LLC

Elka Weber, *The Yankee at the Seder* [Tricycle Press, imprint of Ten Speed Press, 2009]
Illustrated by Adam Gustavson

"Father Answered in Our Place," Oil (SCC only)

Mark Podwal, *Built By Angels* [Harcourt Children's Books, 2009]

"Dormant Golem Covered with Cobwebs in the Attic of Prague Synagogue," Acrylic, gouache, and colored pencil (SCC only)

Uri Shulevitz, *When I Wore My Sailor Suit* [Farrar, Straus, and Giroux, 2009]

*"After a long voyage, I land on a sunny island," Watercolor; © 2009 by Uri Shulevitz. Used by permission of Farrar, Straus and Giroux, LLC

Laurel Snyder, *Baxter: The Pig Who Wanted to Be Kosher* [Tricycle Press, imprint of Ten Speed Press, 2010]
Illustrated by David Goldin

"I want to be kosher, explained Baxter, so that I can be part of Shabbat dinner," Mixed media (SCC and NYBC)

"Who said anything about being eaten?" Mixed media (SCC and NYBC)

"It says so right here. It is a mitzvah to welcome a stranger," Mixed media (SCC and NYBC)

Daniel Pinkwater, *Beautiful Yetta: The Yiddish Chicken* [Feiwel & Friends, 2010]
Illustrated by Jill Pinkwater
*"I'm Free!" Marker, pen and ink; Text © 2010 by Daniel Pinkwater; Illustrations © 2010 by Jill Pinkwater. Used with the permission of Macmillan Children's Publishing Group.
"The streets of Brooklyn are strange to Yetta," Marker, pen and ink
"The truck rumbles through the darkness," Marker, pen and ink (SCC and NYBC)
"Mr. Flegleman begins to unload the crates," Marker, pen and ink (SCC and NYBC)
"One of the chickens is brave and clever," Marker, pen and ink (SCC and NYBC)

Eric A. Kimmel, *Joha Makes a Wish: A Mideastern Tale*, [Marshall Cavendish Corporation, 2010]
Illustrated by Omar Rayyan
"The poor animal didn't like being carried any more than Joha liked carrying her," Watercolor (SCC only)
"He hadn't gone far when he encountered a procession coming down the main street," Watercolor (SCC only)

COLLATERAL MATERIALS

Production artwork and film assets from DreamWorks' SHREK films; [1995–present] Courtesy of DreamWorks Animation (SCC and NYBC)
Where the Wild Things Are Storybook Figures [McFarlane Toys, 2000]
"Tzippy," "Max and Goat Boy," "Aaron," "Moishe," "Emil," "Bernard," Plastic, printer paper; Courtesy of the Skirball Museum, Skirball Cultural Center; Gift of Terrence Fitzgerald (SCC and NYBC)

Max Records as Max, Forest Whitaker as Ira and Catherine O'Hara as Judith in Warner Bros. Pictures', Legendary Pictures' and Village Roadshow Pictures' film "Where the Wild Things Are," a Warner Bros. Pictures release, 2009; Digital print

James Gandolfini as Carol and Max Records as Max in Warner Bros. Pictures', Legendary Pictures' and Village Roadshow Pictures' film "Where the Wild Things Are," a Warner Bros; Pictures release, 2009; Photograph by Matt Nettheim; Digital print

Max Records as Max and Paul Dano as Alexander in Warner Bros. Pictures', Legendary Pictures' and Village Roadshow Pictures' film "Where the Wild Things Are," a Warner Bros. Pictures release, 2009; Digital print

Max Records as Max in Warner Bros. Pictures', Legendary Pictures' and Village Roadshow Pictures' film "Where the Wild Things Are," a Warner Bros. Pictures release, 2009; Photograph by Matt Nettheim; Digital print; Courtesy of Warner Bros. Pictures

Curious George Memorabilia, [1997–2009]
Courtesy of Universal Partnerships & Licensing. CG Classic: ™ & © HMH. CG Film: ™ & © Universal Studios and/or HMH. CG TV: ™ & © Universal Studios and / or HMH (SCC only)